Unlocking the Power of *The Secret*

*10 Key steps
to transform your
thoughts and life*

Ruth L. Miller

Unlocking the Power of *The Secret:* 10 key steps to transform your thoughts and life
© 2020 by Ruth L Miller

Published by Portal Center Press
Oregon, USA
www.portalcenterpress.com

ISBN: 978-1-936902-33-0

Ebook ISBN: 978-1-936902-22-4

For all the powerful beings who feel "stuck" and are sure there's a key, somewhere, to free them from the limits holding them back.

Contents

Foreword i
Introduction 1
Key One: Observation 3
   Discovering What We Believe 7
   Discovering What We Expect 10
   Discovering What We Desire 11
   Discovering What Drives Us 14
Key Two: Contemplation 17
   Discovering the Patterns 19
Key Three: Expression 21
   Experiencing the Feelings 23
   Pressing Feelings from the Inside Out 25
Key Four: Release 29
Key Five: Creation 33
   Our Creative Nature 33
   Creating a New Life 35
   Creating a New Mental Framework 36
   Steps along the Way 39
   Creating Through Imagination 43
Key Six: Affirmation 45
   Writing affirmations is a science. 45
Key Seven: Iteration 47
Key Eight: Discernment 51

    Not Analysis.. 51
    Not Judgment 52
    Learning to Discern... 53
    $E_f \Leftrightarrow 3E$.. 54
    Knowing whether it "fits"................................. 55
    Knowing when to quit...................................... 59
Key Nine: Enjoyment 61
    Abraham's Contribution to the The Secret...... 61
    Other Inspirations for The Secret 63
Key Ten: Love & Appreciation 67

Author's Biography 69

Foreword

Whether or not you've seen the movie *The Secret* or read Rhonda Byrnes' books, you've probably seen people who, somehow, seem to live almost magical lives. And if you're like most folks, seeing what's possible wakes you up to wanting to live that way, too.

Most of the time, such people have no idea why their lives are so good; they're too busy enjoying them to stop and figure it out. But every now and then someone will be living that life because they've learned how to – and they're the ones who can teach the rest of us what it takes.

The authors who've been quoted and referred to in the pages that follow are people who've come from difficult circumstances into a life of joy, satisfaction, and fulfillment, and then have shared their insights with the rest of us.

In these few pages, I've pulled together parts of the core of their teachings. You may want to explore their writings more fully in my Library of Hidden Knowledge series published (Beyond Words, a division of Simon & Schuster/Atria, their website is: www.beyondword.com).

Many of my students (and website readers; mine is www.ruthlmillerphd.com) will recognize my "accept-express-release-replace" process, also known as Ruth's "releasing the past" method, in these pages. That's because it's the most complete and effective process I know to no longer be weighed down by the burdens of past experiences and begin to live a higher-frequency, fulfilling present.

> *How can we hope to choose joy when our past patterns have blinded us to the opportunities?*

Once we've let them go, though, a whole new world of possibilities opens up – a world in which joy is the norm, appreciation is the mechanism that keeps things unfolding in greater delight, and fulfillment is the outcome.

My hope is that you'll use the keys that are offered here to find yours.

Introduction

The Key to the success illustrated in the film *The Secret* is not in the words we say but in the thoughts we think about our self and the world around us. And those aren't just the surface thoughts – the affirmations, the chants, the statements of intention – that we read or hear ourselves thinking and saying. No, the Law of Attraction draws on the deep feelings and beliefs that we hold about who we are and how the world works, which are hidden underneath our waking thoughts.

In today's media-enhanced world, though, hearing those thoughts and beliefs, much less changing them, takes more than a few affirmations.

Our eyes and ears are constantly being bombarded with all kinds of thoughts evoking and reinforcing all kinds of deeply buried feelings.

As a result most of us hold conflicting ideas about different aspects of ourselves and our lives. In one moment we think the world is wonderful and in another that it's awful; or that our family loves us and then that they mistreat us; or that we have all the ability we need to have the life we want, and then that we haven't got a clue. As one of my students said while we were considering the conflicting thoughts behind her recent series of headaches, "that's it in a nutshell: part of me believes 'I'm okay, just fine;' another part says I'm definitely not okay!"

Changing these deep beliefs is an ongoing process that involves several steps. We begin with observation and move through contemplation, expression, release, creation, and *then* affirmation.

All this can happen instantly, in a flash of recognition and insight. But for most of us, most of the time, it happens gradually, layer by layer, as we discover what we truly believe, see how those beliefs no longer serve us, and find the way to be done with them so we can move on and become the powerfully loving, creative beings we were born to be.

This book is a guide to that process.

It's the key to the real power of *The Secret,* built on the experiences and understandings of the many teachers and philosophers whose ideas were used in the book and film by Rhonda Byrne, as well as on my own experience and the experience of my students. The process is simple, once we learn how to do it.

Until then, we bounce back and forth in a world that seems to give us everything we ask for one day and nothing we could ever desire the next. After that, though, the world becomes a wonderful playground, with delight-filled challenges and possibilities galore!

🗝 Key One: Observation

Most of us are in the habit of ignoring most of what's going on inside and around us. We tend to focus on a task or a person, or some worry, fear, or concern, rather than really looking at the people, places, and things in our world – much less the thoughts and feelings we're experiencing in the moment.

It's easy to ignore what's in our minds and not demanding our attention, but we pay a price when we do so, and usually that price is our health and wellbeing.

One of the most useful ideas I've encountered in my studies of psychology and cybernetics is that of the Mental Framework. We all have one.

Every being on this planet perceives life through a set of filters based on their genetics, environment, and history. A reptile's brain is wired in a certain way so that it will perceive, and act on, the world around it to maximize nutrition and safety for itself and its offspring. A bird's brain does so with a wider range of perspective. A dog or other mammal's brain is wired to do all that and more: it includes responding to the emotions and behaviors of its pack and others it relates to. A human's brain includes all of those and also the ability to make value judgments and long-range plans, to draw inferences about the larger world from a small set of information, and to create.

So, when a human being observes something, we're not just using our eyes and ears and other senses. We're also bringing all of our Mental Framework to the moment – including all our past observations and inherited tendencies – of which the ones with the greatest emotional intensity attached to them count the most.

We all have a mind-filter in front of our eyes, so we rarely see what's actually happening in the moment.

Instead, we see some combination of what our senses are taking in and all the emotional connections it brings up for us. You know how it is: smell a turkey roasting and you're remembering holiday meals; see police lights flashing behind you and in your mind you're already being pulled over; hear a baby scream and you're sure the worst has happened; hear a tune and you're remembering the situation that made it important to you.

Lots of neurological studies being done these days support this understanding of how our minds work, but the important thing to remember is that what we experience is not nearly as much "out there" as "in here."

Back in the 1970s, Self Improvement had moved from articles in magazines and books to weekend seminars. One of the first and best known of these was developed by a man called Werner Erhardt. He pulled together a wide range of teachings from many sources, ranging from Zen Buddhism to the work of L. Ron Hubbard, founder of Scientology. The seminars were called e.s.t. and, for many people, these events were the first time they'd ever been invited to really look at the choices they made in their lives and the reasons for those choices. The weekends were an intense, often difficult experience for almost everyone who went through them, but the payoff for most people was that for the first time in their lives they began making conscious choices based on what they really wanted from life, rather than simply playing and replaying the old "programs" they'd adopted and adapted from their parents, schools, churches, and workplaces.

Since then, e.s.t. has evolved into Landmark, and thousands of other "wake-up weekend" programs have been developed with hundreds of thousands of people going through them, all over the world.

In all of them, the first step is simply to observe how your life is working and what role your own choices play in that.

Then, just like Dr. Phil on tv, the leader usually asks "... and how's that working for you?" and gives you the opportunity to make a conscious choice about your life.

Long before the 1970s, though, men and women across the U.S. and Europe were asking similar questions. They rarely talked about them in public, but they would spend long evenings in front of the fireplace exploring whether life had to be lived the way they were told, or if there was another way.

Henry David Thoreau was among the first Americans to write about these questions, in his famous book *Walden Pond*. He had persuaded his neighbor and mentor, the great Transcendentalist, Ralph Waldo Emerson, to let him build a cabin on Emerson's 11-acre "pond." He wanted to try an experiment in living by choice, close to Nature, rather than following society's expectations. Emerson, who in his essay *Self Reliance* encourages everyone to live by what our intuition, rather than our society, tells us, was happy to oblige. The result was a veritable manual on conscious observation and choice that remains a classic today. Emerson was delighted, and in my book *Natural Abundance*, I "translated" the following from that essay:

> If you can live your own life fully and follow the guidance of your heart, then you shall bring forth a wonderful, uniquely original expression of divine Creativity.

So insist on yourself; never imitate....
When you do the things that are yours to do, it's not possible to do too much or hope too much.[1]

To learn to live from inner guidance, rather than society's "programs" is an essential key to living an abundant life.

But, as both Emerson and Thoreau said, over 150 years ago, our culture has trained us to follow the voice of authority as expressed by others, so most of us have no idea how to proceed.

Discovering What We Believe

One of the more profound teachings from these teachers, as well as gestalt therapy, e.s.t., and Scientology, was "if you want to know what you intended, look at your results." It can also be stated as

"if you want to know what you believe, look at your circumstances."

Most of us really have no clue as to what we truly believe. We know what we were taught to say we believe—whether in church or in school or in our families—but behind that stated belief are several

---

[1] This quote, like all the others in this book, is from the Library of Hidden Knowledge series, in which I took the writings of 19th century philosophers and "translated" them for the 21st century reader, and included the author's original in the back. This one is from *Natural Abundance, Ralph Waldo Emerson's Guide to Prosperity*, the essay called "Self Reliance".

layers of assumptions, ideas, and expectations that, taken together, make up what may be a very different set of beliefs from the ones we can state out loud. In church, for example, how many people speak of an "all-loving God" and then talk about the great punishments that God will hand out to the sinful. Or, in science: how many people say they know the earth travels around the sun but talk about the sun "rising" and "setting" on a day-to-day basis? In our families, we may say we love our siblings or parents, but how many of us have, at some point in our lives, deliberately done something we know will lead to one of our family members' distress? And many of us say that we believe people should be honest, but are not willing to state what we really want or what we really think about someone else.

In fact, we often say we believe one thing and then act on a different set of beliefs, entirely.

So, how do we find out what we actually believe?

Look around.

Look at your circumstances. What parts of your life go smoothly, with few problems, difficulties, or stressors? These are the reflections of your beliefs that are clear and conflict free. If they're in alignment with what you think you want, they're also reflecting your belief that you are good, or capable, or supported, or provided-for.

What parts of your life are not at all what you think you want? These are also reflections of what you believe about the world and yourself – and they're also reflections of your beliefs that you can't have what you want, or that you have to do just the right thing to get what you want, or that you're not capable, or not supported, supplied, or provided for.

What parts of your life are really out of line – just not at all what you think you deserve or could ever have brought on to yourself? These are the reflections of your beliefs that you are not in control of your life, that someone, somewhere "out there" has the means to make your life whatever "they" think it should be, whenever they're inclined to, with little or no say on your part.

Most of us live a mixture of circumstances because we have a mix of beliefs. We do well in some areas of life; not so well in others. We easily make some things happen; not at all others. And it's this mixture that brings us a life that is both wonderful and awful at the same time – or that seems to oscillate between the 2 states: big highs followed by deep lows. Our life experience begins to look something like the graph below, with brief moments of delight and appreciation, and lots of climbing out of the depths in between.

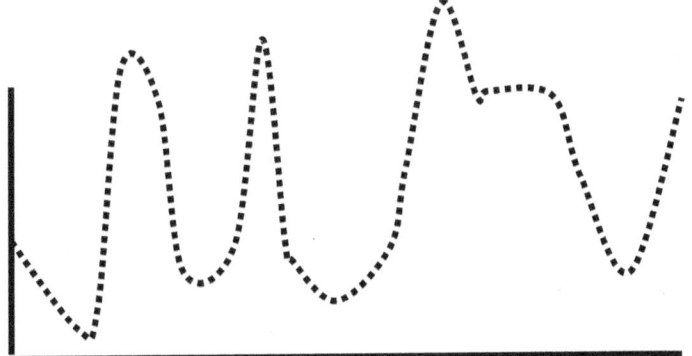

> *Our mixture of beliefs leads us to a mixture of experiences and also to invite a mix of events and people into our lives.*

Discovering What We Expect

Think about it: how often do you go out the door in the morning (or whenever) worrying about how things are going to turn out? How much of your time do you wonder if it's going to rain or if that project you've been working on is about to fall apart or if that memo from the boss is a punishment or if the people you care about are all right or if the government is going to do something to you or to the world?

Most of us have a stream of thought running through our minds all the time, and that stream is filled with thoughts about what we're afraid might happen, or about what we're not doing right, or what someone else is not doing right, most of the time. Those thoughts are telling us what we believe about ourselves and our world.

Now, imagine you're planning a vacation. What do you think about? Are you filled with thoughts of how wonderful you're going to feel? How beautiful it will be? How nice the people you'll be with are? Or are you concerned about the weather, how people will get along, whether you'll have enough money, etc.? Chances are that you do a bit of both – another indicator of mixed beliefs. Now remember your last vacation. Was it pure heaven? Or was it a mixture of nice and not-so-nice? Whatever it was is a function of your beliefs, and the thoughts and feelings that stem from them.

If you walk into a room expecting to be noticed and appreciated, you'll hold your head a little higher, you'll catch peoples' eye and smile more often – and you'll see people respond in like ways. The same applies the other way: when you expect to be ignored and unwanted you'll hold your head down, not quite meeting peoples' eyes, not really smiling – and people will respond accordingly. Try it some time and see.

This principle applies to every aspect of our lives. We show up with our expectations as obvious as the clothes we're wearing, and the world responds accordingly. As Emerson famously said, "who you are... speaks so loudly that I cannot hear a word you say"[2]

The most effective way to discover our expectations is to look at what we see and have in our world each day.

Discovering What We Desire

We live in a culture that constantly presents us with desirable objects and ways of living – and through the genius of marketing, we're often convinced we really need something that, 10 minutes before, we didn't even know existed. In such a world, knowing what we truly desire is not always easy. As Emerson reminded us in his famous essay *Nature*:

---

[2] From the Library of Hidden Knowledge series, *Natural Abundance. Ralph Waldo Emerson's Guide to Prosperity*, the essay "Spiritual Laws", p. 20.

The hunger for wealth fools the eager pursuer. What's the goal? Surely it's to have more experiences of beauty and comfort, safe from any distressing intrusions, but what a complex process to attain a simple end! ... For most wealth seekers, having riches was good at first. It fed the body, delighted the senses, silenced the creaking door, and brought friends together in a warm and pleasant room. Sadly, though, in an effort to acquire these, the primary purpose is too often forgotten, and the means become the end.... [3]

Most of us, therefore, end up owning things that don't really serve us.

We end up joining groups we don't really feel like we belong in, living in places that don't really feel like home, and eating foods that don't really nourish us.

Fortunately, we *can* discover what we truly desire. There are a few easy guidelines to use, and we can apply them to things we currently have as well as to things the world seems to be offering us.

First is the physical response: when you actually hold the item, embrace the person, or taste the food, does your heart sing? Does your body relax and say "aaah!"? Or do you feel some tension, find your mind wandering, or seek some distraction?

Second is the values test. Ask yourself: "Does this item, person, or experience conform to what I want to see more of in my life and world? Does it contribute

---

[3] From the Library of Hidden Knowledge series, *Natural Abundance. Ralph Waldo Emerson's Guide to Prosperity*, p. 10.

to the world I want to live in? Or does it in some way cause harm or distress? Another way to put it is: is this loving, helpful, beautiful, and harmonious with the life I want to live?"

For both of these, some of the work that was done in the 1970s is helpful. It's called visualization, and with it, you can test something by imagining being with or holding or tasting it, almost as effectively as when you have it physically there.

If you don't believe you can visualize, try to remember your bedroom: what color are the walls? The bedspread? The floor? Where is your dresser? See! You <u>can</u> use your inner vision!

At first it may seem strange or difficult to be able to imagine something so strongly that your body reacts. But just think for a while about the monster under the bed or in the t (or the possibility of a cop car behind you while you're speeding along) and you'll see how easy it is for the body to respond to an imagined situation. If you want more detailed guidelines, you can check out Shakti Gawain's *Creative Visualization* or Robert Masters' and Jean Houston's *Mind Games,* both of which provide detailed guidelines and scripts for developing our ability to sense fully what we've imagined.

Visualization is also helpful in discovering what we really do want when everything that's offered doesn't feel right. We simply allow ourselves to feel what it feels like to have everything the way that feels best to us, and then sense what the elements are in that imagined situation. We can then compare what feels good in our imagination with what is being offered and perhaps create a new alternative in the process.

For example we might imagine waking up in the most comfortable, pleasant surroundings possible, then "see" what that looks like, "feel" what that feels like, "hear" what that sounds like, etc. As we do this over and over, both the scene and our ability to sense it evolves and changes, and the choices that have been made from our programming gradually give way to our true desires.

Discovering What Drives Us

All of us have memories of experiences that we'd rather not have to repeat. Most of us have memories, usually from childhood, of experiences that were so intense or happened so often, that we decided that was the way we must be and how the world must be.

Many of us don't remember those experiences, because we've been taught they don't mean anything in our lives as adults.

Well, since Sigmund Freud discovered the effectiveness of psychoanalysis back at the end of the 19th century, the idea that what we experience as children doesn't matter has been proven again and again to be false.

In fact, all of us are making choices every day based on the images and feelings we carry from our childhood.

It's like those shows where the adults are sitting around a table and someone says something and suddenly everyone at the table is a child again, reacting as they did at 5 or 8 or 10; we all act as if we were the age when those events happened far more often than we realize. One way to observe this is to go to your parents' home and watch how everyone's behavior changes by the second or third day. Almost always, everyone slips back into the behavior patterns that were "normal" when you lived together before. This is especially visible at holidays.

> *Another way to discover what's driving you is to observe the experiences you've had over and over in life.*

They're common in our culture: dating or choosing as friends the same kind of people, even when you thought "this time it will be different"; losing or forgetting important clients or meetings; flubbing important deadlines; taking on far more responsibility than the job description requires (and then going unrewarded for all that extra work); having accidents like spills or fender-benders or falls, or breaking furniture when you're about to have a good time or meet someone important. These are the obvious kinds of behaviors we can observe, and they're illustrated (and explained) beautifully in the wedding-reception scene in the video *What the Bleep Do We Know?*

Less obvious examples of this process include: breaking resolutions and other promises to yourself; choosing foods that you believe are not good for the body; being suddenly too tired or too sick when something pleasurable or potentially important is about to happen; letting someone else's idea of what's good be more important than your own... and many more like them.

Whenever we make a destructive choice or find ourselves in an unpleasant situation that we've experienced more than once before, we can count on it; this is the current manifestation of a pattern, an old decision that's now one of our programs. More, the greater the upset we experience about the situation, the younger and more determined we were when we made that decision.

So what's driving our actions in this moment is almost always the buried-but-powerful decisions we made early on in our lives that have defined what's "normal" for us.

Human beings tend to recreate and maintain what we feel is "normal", so we will do and say and invite into our lives whatever recreates or maintains the pattern resulting from that decision.

This means that we need to observe the pattern – in our actions, in our experiences, and in our circumstances – because to know what we believe, all we need to do is observe our situation.

🗝 Key Two: Contemplation

The ancient Greeks and Romans held the idea that to "Know Yourself" was the most important thing a person could do. In our culture, though, we're encouraged to focus on everyone and everything except ourselves. Many of us have even been taught that such introspection is at best a wasted effort and at worst, a sin.

James Allen, who launched the self-help movement in 1912 with his book *As A Man Thinketh*, definitely did not accept that point of view. Instead, he suggested,

> ... when we can reflect on our condition and search diligently for the laws of cause and effect that govern our being, it's possible to discover them within ourselves. Then we become wise, directing our energies with intelligence and managing our thoughts for desired results. ...
>
> As gold and diamonds are obtained through much searching and mining, we can find every truth connected with our being if we're willing to dig deep into the mine of our own minds.[4]

To sit quietly and "do nothing" is not always easy. In our culture we've been taught that not doing something is being lazy, and if we've been caught

---

[4] From the Library of Hidden Knowledge series, *As We Think, So We Are*, James Allen's guide to transforming our thoughts and lives, p.

"daydreaming" we've been told we weren't ok – possibly even mentally disturbed. But how can we hope to understand something if we don't stop and think about it?

> **How can we hope to understand ourselves if we don't stop and contemplate what we do, why we do it, and what we might choose to do differently?**

Seeing what works and doesn't work is a powerful step in the direction of transforming our lives – and it's ongoing, too. As long as we're occupying these bodies, we'll find things that we decided when we were much younger playing out in our lives today. The good news is, having seen the pattern we can begin to undo the power of it and live from different choices, instead.

Still, we've lived to this point based on those patterns, and life isn't *entirely* awful. We have bodies that function; relationships of a sort; means to get by day-to-day. So we don't want to just get rid of all the old patterns. We need to be clear about what works for us and what doesn't.

In his essay *Self Reliance*, Emerson said "a foolish consistency is the hobgoblin of little minds."[5]

Note that he said "foolish" consistency is the problem. He's talking about allowing ourselves to repeat the same thing over and over simply because we (or the people who taught us) always have.

---

[5] From the Library of Hidden Knowledge series *Natural Abundance, Ralph Waldo Emerson's Guide for Prosperity*, pp. 198 & 74.

Discovering the Patterns

To make that choice and begin to really understand the patterns of our life we need to spend time contemplating it.

We need to ask ourselves some questions.

Here's a few to consider:
- When did this start?
- Who was involved?
- How do I feel about them?
- What do I wish they'd done differently?
- What was I thinking?
- What did I think I was doing?
- What would I do differently if I could?
- How do I feel about me?
- How would I like to change this?

It's a good idea to take some time and write some of your answers down – either on the computer or on paper – so you can begin to gain some perspective on this pattern, on the decisions involved, on the people involved, and on what you want to change. You may even want to draw a diagram, connecting certain events and people.

Focus on just one pattern at a time. If it's a series of relationships that somehow always turned out the same way, go back as far as you can to the first time you remember feeling that way (probably with a parent; maybe a sibling). Later you can look at other parts of your life. If the pattern is a tendency to undermine yourself, remember as many times that you've done so as you can until you find a time when someone told you something about yourself that you decided must be true. For each pattern, ask all of the questions in the list above for each time you experienced it. And write the answers down.

As you do so, you'll discover several things. One, you'll begin to understand things about you and your life you didn't know were possible to understand. Second, you'll begin to see how much your own choices have brought you into the experiences you've had. And third, you'll start having emotions you didn't know were there – or were anywhere near that intense!

And that's what the next Key helps us deal with.

🗝 Key Three: Expression

The decisions we made in childhood are attached to emotions that may have been buried since the moment we made that decision. And every time events related to those decisions happen, the original emotions are brought just below the surface of our awareness, while new ones are being added to them.

In this culture, most of us are trained not to express emotions.

When children are sad we tell them "it's all right, you don't have to cry." When they hurt, we tell them "it doesn't hurt that much." When they're angry we make it clear that their behavior is just not ok. And when they're afraid we tell them there's nothing to be afraid of.

You can see how we got the message that we can't either trust or express our feelings. In fact, through these and other messages, most of us were given permission to express only happy feelings, and those only in small, relatively quiet ways.

Yet all of us feel all those feelings!

A friend of mine who'd been trained not to express his feelings in childhood and was experiencing some real distress as an adult went to a therapist who gave him a list, telling him that in any given moment he was always feeling one or more of the feelings on that list. They were:

- ➤ *sad*
- ➤ *mad*
- ➤ *glad*
- ➤ *hungry*
- ➤ *tired*
- ➤ *afraid*

What a great list! All of the thousands of words in the English language for feelings and emotions come down to that! And we're all feeling one or more of them all the time!

I would add only 2 more to that list

- ➤ *loving*
- ➤ *loved*

When we're feeling loved or loving, most of the other feelings are greatly lessened – we're rarely angry when we're feeling loving or loved, and how many of us feel hungry when we're in love? Henry Drummond would, I think, agree. In my book *One Law,* I "translated" part of his marvelous little book *The Greatest Thing* as:

> Why do you want to live tomorrow? For most of us, we want to see someone tomorrow who loves us and we want to be with them and love them back....
>
> People commit suicide when they think there's no one to love them. So long as they have friends who love them and whom they love, they will live, because to live is to love. If it's only the love of a dog, it will keep a person living; but let that

go and there's no contact with life, no reason to live. The energy of life has failed.[6]

So, with all the other feelings we have, feeling loved and loving is basic – and, sadly, often made difficult or impossible by the social norms in our culture.

Experiencing the Feelings

Most of us in this culture were trained not only to not express our feelings, but to believe that even feeling them was dangerous! We were told about people who were overcome with rage or sadness or fear and went out and did terrible things to other people – and themselves.

> *Through stories, we were taught that to even allow a little upset feelings to show was "unmanly," "unloving," "cowardly," and worse.*

Some of us were punished for having those feelings. Others were sent to therapy and medicated.

And yet, when we don't allow those feelings to be experienced and expressed, they continue to bind us to those decisions we made when we felt them as children – and worse, they continue to be stored in the body in ways that typically cause harmful or even painful symptoms.

That may sound farfetched, but think about it. What happens to your body when you're happy? What happens when you're stressed? What happens

---

[6]m the Library of Hidden Knowledge series, *One Law*, p. 30.

when you're struggling with some issue? What happens when you're fighting someone or something? You know your body is affected; you can feel it!

Well, apply that over days and months and years and imagine what's happening to the parts of your body that are affected.

> *Day after day, the chemicals that the biologist Candace Pert described as "molecules of emotion" are sent to parts of your body to help you fight or be strong or run away.*

And day after day they're not used. So the cells change. The chemicals are stored in various parts of the body. The glands that release those chemicals are depleted.

In time, the body starts exhibiting more serious symptoms. Usually it starts with achiness, colds, and flu, as the cells are out of alignment or not strong enough to repel viruses. Then there might be ongoing fatigue, more pains in more places... and so forth.

The body is not a pretty picture after a few years of suppression. And, in fact, our bodies are such a perfect record of our emotional experiences that Caroline Myss, author of *Why People Don't Heal and How They Can* has said "our biology is our biography."

So how do those of us who've been so thoroughly trained not to feel our feelings, actually allow ourselves to experience them?

Safely!

Pressing Feelings from the Inside Out

At this point we have discovered the pattern and contemplated the experiences associated with it, and have written our answers to the questions in Key Two, above. The next step is to set aside a time and place where no one else will be affected by whatever we decide to do or say, or whatever noise we might make in the process.

Going through it for the first time may take a while, so schedule as much of a weekend (or equivalent) as you can for it. You will want to be in a safe place with some place to rest, some place to move freely, some intense music, and something to write on. Make sure you have something to eat and drink on hand, too – and lots of water to replenish and cleanse with.

This is a powerful process, and you will definitely see results.

For it to be most effective, though, it's important to focus on just one pattern – doing so makes dealing with others easier, later.

For most of us, the very act of expressing emotions is so foreign we really have to work ourselves up to do so. This is where writing the memories down beforehand is helpful; they make it easy to go back over the pattern and its experiences and think about all the people involved, which, usually will begin to open us up to the feelings we've been suppressing, repressing, and storing in the body.

The word "express", derived from the Latin, can be interpreted as "press from". Juice is "expressed" from fruit. Many people describe suddenly experiencing sadness or a memory when some muscles are pressed while having a massage.

> *So expressing our feelings is a process of "pushing from" our bodies, as well as our emotional center and our intellect, all the words, images, thoughts, and movements that are associated with the pattern.*

We do this first by saying or writing all the things we never said about those experiences – or we may have said but it wasn't heard.

We may speak or yell or even scream those previously unsaid words as we feel them. As we start to feel the feelings we may move our bodies, swinging our arms and legs, dancing or punching out (on a pillow or mattress) some of the intensity of what's been stored in our muscles. Or we use other kinds of movement, like throwing pillows across the room or throwing rocks into the ocean or river. We might do what one of my teachers used to encourage, and get a short length of garden-hose and hit some old phone-directories or stacks of magazines in order to let the body finally use the muscles that have been holding onto those feelings all this time.

> *All of this is done in a safe place away from people who might be*

> *disturbed by our doing so – and we do it for as long as we can stand doing it.*

Ah, the joys of expression! Freedom! It's no longer stuck inside, but out there! Finally, after all these years, we've said and done all the things we didn't think we could!

And it's literally exhausting. All that intense feeling drains the body's reserves.

So we know we're done with this phase when we feel physically and emotionally drained, almost too tired and empty to do anything at all. We find ourselves saying "and I know you really were doing the best you could... trying to love me..." or some such understanding or compassionate words.

Sometimes we actually curl up and fall asleep at this point, or at least go into a deep dream-like state, while the body recovers from this sudden pushing out of what has been stored so long, and the mind lets go of it as well. Or we just lie there feeling drained.

For some, this is a time of deep peace – perhaps their first such experience in years.

There. It is done. It is no longer hidden in the body-mind. Now we can begin again – with the next, equally important, phase of the process.

Key Four: Release

At this point the process is only partially complete. Our emotional burden isn't fully gone yet. It's as if we've dumped a load of garbage in the room and now we need to get it out of there.

What we're doing is changing our Mental Framework, and that means we have to make a clear and clean cut away from what has been "normal."

When we've reached the point where the only emotion we can pull up is something like "I'm done; it's over; I wish it had never happen; I know it could have been different..." it's time to release and let go of the whole set of ideas, feelings, and memories that are associated with the pattern we've been focusing on.

Doing this effectively – separating the feelings and ideas we've expressed from our sense of our "normal" self – is a process of releasing and letting go. We need to dissolve the old Mental Framework, take it apart and remove all that we've expressed from our being.

But this may not be a simple process. After all, we've hung on to some of our beliefs and fears for a very long time!

Writing all our feelings about our experiences and the people involved, then tearing up the paper we've written on into tiny pieces and burning it is a good start. Watching the words be transformed into light and ash helps our minds get the message that this is no longer important. And where fire isn't possible, dissolving the paper in water is almost as effective.

One student imagined putting everyone involved in a hot air balloon and watching it drift out of sight. Another wrote a couple words on a big rock, carried it to a nearby bridge and threw it over the railing, watching it splash into the river below.

Florence Scovel Shinn, in *The Game of Life and How to Play It,* called this "Casting the Burden."

> I knew a woman whose burden was resentment. For years, resentment had held her in a state of torment and imprisoned her soul, her subconscious mind. She worked with me for several sessions and learned to say, with feeling, "I cast this burden of resentment on the Christ within, and I go free, to be loving, harmonious, and happy." As she did so, as she felt the release of these once cherished resentments, the Almighty superconscious flooded the subconscious with love for the people she had formerly resented and her whole life was changed.[7]

Clearly, Shinn's student was a Christian who believed the New Testament suggestion to cast our burden on Jesus. It's a powerful tool for millions of people.

---

[7] From the Library of Hidden Knowledge series, *The New Game of Life,* chapter 6: "Casting the Burden".

It may not be that simple for us, however. We may not be comfortable with the idea of a higher power that can do things for us we can't do for ourselves. Or we may need something that we can *feel* as well as say.

My version of that is to put all the feelings and ideas and memories associated with the pattern in a big bag, roll it up the ramp of an imaginary rocket ship, count down to lift-off, then watch the ship soar into the sun and be transformed into healing light.

Whatever method we use, we combine visualization and a physical sensation to help the body-mind know that it is free of this pattern.

And when we feel that freedom, the realization that it really is no longer part of who we are, we can get up and take a shower and wash all the residue of these feelings – and the experiences associated with them – from the body. Sometimes it helps to imagine that a stream of light is flowing through the water, through the top of the head and down through the body, washing away all the residue of these feelings from inside, as well as out. We feel the letting-go; we watch it all flow down the drain.

Now we can say "It is done! I've released this pattern and I'm ready to create a new life!"

Key Five: Creation

Like dry sand falling back into a hole we've dug at the beach, feelings and memories tend to drift back into their old familiar niches in our minds. So, now that we've released what no longer serves us, we have to fill that hole with something as firm as concrete to keep it from pouring back in. Having released those old patterns, we now must replace them with a new one.

And that involves creating a new idea of self – one that no longer includes the old pattern.

Our Creative Nature

Across cultures it's understood at a deep level that, unlike other creatures, human beings respond to the world creatively. In our culture, made up mostly of what's been called the "people of the Book" – Jews, Muslims, and Christians – humanity is understood to have been created in the Creator's likeness or nature. In other cultural traditions, it's explained in different ways, but the message is the same.

Think about it. We're always creating – what we're wearing, our homes, our workplaces, our food, yards, toys,

We're always taking something and making it our own, or making it to look like something else, or dreaming

up a different way of doing things. It's our essential nature.

That's why, when we use our creative ability, we feel great. We have a sense of accomplishment, of fulfillment. The lives of artists, musicians, actors, and dancers illustrate this point – as do the lives of the people we observe every day, in the kitchen, the garden, or at work.

And when we don't use our creative capacity, when we fall into a habit of just accepting what comes our way and not creating something unique, we begin to fall apart, emotionally and physically. We can see this in the lives of the great artists, of course; there are many stories of the "agony and ecstasy" of the creative life. But we can also see it in our own lives and in the lives of those around us, if we stop and consider.

In fact, people generally feel uncomfortable about creating things only if they've been raised in an environment where an authority's rules or social norms were considered most important, or where their creative offerings were criticized, judged, or discounted too many times (psychologists say it only takes 59% of the time for a response to be seen as "true").

Even then, though, we'll usually find some niche, some area of expertise, where the judges and critics haven't got anything to say, and we'll express our creative nature in that. Children who were told they couldn't draw often become musicians or planners or software designers; adults who believe they haven't "a creative bone in their body" find new ways to prepare foods or solve problems at work or fix their cars.

> *We're always creating something.*
> *And that's a good thing.*

Creating a New Life

In this culture, based largely on the Bible, with its description of a world run by an all-powerful Creator, one of the most important-yet-difficult realizations any human being can have is that no one "out there" is creating our life for us.

> *We are, with each choice we*
> *make, setting ourselves up for the*
> *consequences of that choice.*

As the Christian Bible puts it "we reap what we sow". Emerson said, in his essay *Compensation:*

> From all perspectives, everything is perfectly interconnected …
>
> So cause and effect, means and ends, seeds and fruit cannot be separated. The effect blooms in the cause; it's the fruit in the seed. Every act rewards itself. Reaction is in the action itself and not in the circumstances surrounding the action.[8]

This understanding is the basis for virtually all of the self-help books that have ever been published. From James Allen's *As A Man Thinketh* to Wallace Wattles' *The Science of Getting Rich* to Charles Haanel's *The Master Key System* to Napoleon Hill's *Think and Grow Rich* to Rhonda Byrne's *The Secret,* all of the teachers

---

[8] From the Library of Hidden Knowledge series, *Natural Abundance, Ralph Waldo Emerson's Guide to Prosperity*, the essay "The Law of Compensation" p. 44.

and writers and speakers who've helped thousands of people begin to live a life of abundance have worked from this premise:

> *We make the choices of what will be said and done and how we will respond, and these choices are the basis for what we will experience in the future.*

The fact is clear. The process is not so clear – until one remembers the Mental Framework.

The Mental Framework we bring to each experience determines our perception of that experience, our response to it, and the choices we will make about it. So, if we want to create a different kind of life, we need to create a different Mental Framework.

This is the essence of the teachings in the self-help books; it's the fundamental act of creation every human must undertake. And this is what we're doing in this book.

Creating a New Mental Framework

We've done the most difficult part already: we've observed some of the patterns that make up our Mental Framework and begun to release them. Now we get to "fill the hole in the sand with concrete" and put new ideas into the Mental Framework so that our perceptions, responses, and choices may be different.

James Allen describes the results of doing this in *As We Think, So We Are*.

Clearly, then, overcoming self [our previous way of thinking and being] is not depriving us of gladness, happiness, and joy. Instead, it's constantly experiencing these delights and living with these joy-filling qualities. Overcoming self is abandoning the lust for enjoyment but not enjoyment itself; it's the destruction of the thirst for pleasure but not pleasure itself.[9]

According to his autobiography, Benjamin Franklin decided to change his life by changing his behavior. He began in his late 20s, when he was returning from England (where he'd sown more than a few "wild oats") to the colonies. His approach was to make a list of all the vices he wanted to eliminate from his character and a list of all the virtues he wanted to integrate into his character, and to mark off on the calendar every day that he avoided the one and did the other. He aimed for 30 continuous days for each item on his list, and started over if he missed a day.

Well, Ben's plan worked for him and he went on to become one of America's most famous inventors, publishers, and statesmen. Modern neurophysiology says that it takes 28-29 days for the brain to change from one neural pattern to another, and he understood that, over 250 years ago.

Almost 150 years later, James Allen developed a similar plan, in his book *Above Life's Turmoil*. It goes something like the following:

---

[9] From the Library of Hidden Knowledge series, *As We Think, So We Are, James Allen's Guide to transforming our lives*, p. 61-2; exercise on p. 134 in that book, p. 38 in this one.

A. Consider the list of thought processes that always lead to distress and misery, listed below. Write the first one in your journal and remember a time you thought, spoke, or acted out of it. Describe that experience on the line below it, then skip a line or two and write the next one, repeating the process for all ten.

1. Lust
2. Hatred
3. Greed
4. Self-indulgence
5. Self-seeking
6. Vanity
7. Pride
8. Doubt
9. Fear-based thinking
10. Delusion

B. Now do the same for the ten qualities that inevitably bring a sense of well-being and peace:

1. Clear focus
2. Patience
3. Humility
4. Surrender
5. Self-reliance
6. Fearlessness
7. Knowledge
8. Wisdom
9. Compassion
10. Love

C. Now, on the line below your description of the last time you used one of the first ten, rewrite the experience as if you had used some of the second set of qualities, instead. [10]

To begin to eliminate the tendency to use the first ten, go to the back of your journal and, on the last double-page spread, make a chart with the ten sor-

---

[10] From the Library of Hidden Knowledge series, *As We Think So We Are, James Allen's Guide to Transforming Our Lives*, p. 134.

row-producing thoughts along one side, followed by the ten peace-fostering qualities. Then write the numbers 1-28 across the top. Draw lines between the numbers, so it will look something like a calendar. Then:

> 1. For twenty-eight days, at the end of each day, simply check off whether you've used that quality that day. If you've used one of the first ten, then go back to the beginning of your journal, put the date at the top of the next blank page and write the experience as you remember it, then rewrite it as it might have happened using the divine qualities instead. Imagine in as great detail as possible, using all your senses (What colors were present? What sounds?
>
> What tastes and odors? What textures?), how it might have been if you had been creating a blessing instead of misery?
>
> 2. Then, each day when you're done, appreciate the experience as a learning opportunity and imagine the possibilities of a life filled with the blessings you've created in your rewriting of the experience. Then go to bed; the process you've done will help to re-wire your subconscious mind as you sleep to focus on blessing more than sorrow tomorrow.

These are powerful tools for building a new habit of thought that's in alignment with your intentions for a new pattern in your life.

Steps along the Way

Allen suggests that there are 3 phases to the process of creating a new Mental Framework.

The first phase is to see the people involved in a new way. The second is to see ourselves in a new way. And the third is to hold a different intention for the life ahead.

The question that immediately comes up at this point is, "How can I see myself and those others in a different way?" And that question is based on another part of the Mental Framework we were given in this culture: the idea that what's done is done and can't be undone.

But that's another idea that science no longer supports, and that no longer serves us. While it's true that we don't yet know how to make spilled milk flow back into the bottle (except by reversing the video), we do know that electrons can reverse time. And we know how to get on with our lives without having a past experience affect our future. We can change the way we experience things; it's all in the Mental Framework.

To do this, imagine one of the people involved in the pattern you've just released. Let yourself see them, not as someone who hurt you or did something you didn't feel good about, but as someone who is a human being, with all that implies. If you have a spiritual tradition, think of them as a beloved of the Creator, just like you and all the rest of humanity.

The person you see in your mind's eye is the person you expect to see when you think of or hear from or encounter them somewhere.

Who would you rather encounter: a beloved being, bathed in the light of love and wisdom? Or whoever you used to think of when you thought of this person? If you're like most people, you'd rather see them as someone you'd enjoy being with.

Now, as you imagine this person, ask yourself:
- Was it fair or helpful of me to hold those negative feelings about this person?
- Did it help me?
- Did it help them?

When you answer these, you will realize that you've been carrying what *A Course in Miracles* calls "a grievance" against this person. You'll see that it doesn't do either of you any good to do so.

So, in your mind's eye, see this person as if they were flooded with love and light and wellbeing. Then, in your imagination, apologize for having thought of them in the old way.

You're acknowledging that you've done your expressing and releasing work. You no longer carry the pattern that includes the grievance and you want them to know it and forgive you for holding that pattern for so long.

The second phase, having come to this understanding, is to use your imagination, your inner vision, to visualize love and light flowing from them and surrounding you. Allow yourself to experience this person releasing you from any grievance *they* may have held toward *you*. Allow yourself to know that there is nothing between you and them but love and light. *Feel* the release that comes with this awareness.

Getting to this point may seem strange at first but is easier as you apply it to each person in your pattern. And the feeling may last a long while, or just a second or so. Either is fine. It doesn't matter how long. The point is that you actually feel a different feeling toward this person, and from this person.

A surprising thing happens in the process: you also feel different about yourself. You're freed of this grievance; you no longer carry this burden; you have been given peace of mind and heart in return for the pattern and grievance you've released.

> *This is what it means to be forgiven: you are "given" peace and love and freedom "for" the pain you've been carrying.*

The third phase, as soon as you feel only the love and light between you and the others involved, is to declare a different intention for your relationship and life from now on. This is the replacing process, where you "fill the hole" that the releasing process left.

> *Your new intention comes from a deep awareness inside you as you feel the new freedom of release.*

Up to now, your relationship has been based on your own internal pattern, which includes one or more grievances you've held against this person and others. But today, having completed this process, you are creating a new pattern, which you can state as a claim, or intention.

Some simple statement makes itself known, based on the high level of love and understanding you're feeling in the moment. It may be very general; something like, "in my life everyone is always helpful and loving." Or more specific, "whatever the appearance may be as we go through life, the love and light we share remains." It may be a reversal of your past experience: "The people in my life *always* support my wellbeing." Or it may be something that makes sense only to you and the person you've just released and been released by – and that's fine!

You've completed the essential process of replacing: you've transformed your inner relationship with the key person associated with this pattern. The only thing left is to do the same thing with each of the other people associated with this pattern. You need to get to the love and light and this new intention with each of them. That's when you'll be able to live your life in a new way.

And when you've done so, go do something wonderful for yourself, just because it gives you joy! You've earned it!

Creating Through Imagination

Many studies have demonstrated the powerful effect an imagined experience has on the body-mind system. The most famous one compared basketball players: those who simply imagined shooting hoops every day for an hour improved almost as much as those who went over to the court and tossed those balls. Later studies showed that people who imagined their bodies eliminating tumors, growths, and mineral deposits often showed remarkable results.

Over the years, many self-help and healing texts have included guided imagery as one of the tools we can use to create our lives. Using our imagination, we begin to make it real to our minds. As Wallace Wattles tells us in *The Science of Getting Rich,* the book that was the primary inspiration for the film *The Secret,*

> You must hold a clear and definite mental picture of what you want; you can't transmit an idea into the substance unless you have it clearly yourself. You must have it before you can give it... See just what you are ready to receive and get a clear mental picture of it as you wish it to look when you get it.[11]

Florence Shinn supports this understanding in *The Game of Life and How to Play it*:

> ...whatever we imagine almost always becomes our circumstance. So to play the Game of Life successfully, we need to learn how to train the imagination. People who train the mind to see only good bring all the good they can imagine into their lives—health, wealth, love, friends, perfect Self-expression—and their highest ideals come into form.[12]

With this understanding we can truly begin the process of consciously creating our lives.

---

[11] From the Library of Hidden Knowledge series, *The New Science of Getting Rich,* p. 45-46.
[12] From the Library of Hidden Knowledge series, *The New Game of Life and How to Play it,* p. 5.

Key Six: Affirmation

At this point, you've done most of the essential work! You've expressed the feelings that were stored and causing distress in the body-mind system. You've released the pattern the supported those feelings. You've allowed yourself to experience the people involved in a new way, beginning to shift your Mental Framework. You've even set an intention for what your life will be like from now on, and begun to visualize what that life might be.

The next thing is to reinforce your new intention whenever old habits of thought (and the experiences associated with them) show up again. We're "rewiring" the mind to follow the new Mental Framework that we've put in place by creating a new habit of thought to replace the old one.

So think of your intention for your new life. Write a sentence or so to describe it. See if you can say it in 5 to 9 words. This will be your new affirmation. It will replace all the things you used to repeat to yourself over and over about how bad things or people or your behaviors were.

Writing affirmations is a science.

Much has been learned over the past couple hundred years about what works and what doesn't. Some of it has to do with how the mind is trained to perceive ideas in our culture. Some of it has to do with the way the Mental Framework works.

So, when you write or repeat an affirmation remember these guidelines:
1. Always use present tense – it's happening Now.
2. Always use the positive form – it IS; they ARE; I DO; I AM.
3. Keep it simple enough to remember and repeat.

The practice of using affirmations is simple: focus on the experience you're using the affirmation to reinforce for 20-30 minutes morning and evening, then repeat the affirmation as often as possible through the day for 28 days (or a month, or a full moon cycle, if you'd rather – both work).

The affirmation is both a reminder of what you've chosen to create for your life and a re-director if you find yourself heading away from that choice - especially if it looks as if the old pattern may be rearing its ugly head.

Other than that, let it go.

This is not about trying to make something happen; this is about re-training the mind so we can stop preventing our desires from becoming our experience.

It's about thinking in the certain way that will bring about the life we love to live.

Key Seven: Iteration

Have you ever watched a baby learn to walk? Or seen an athlete learn a new skill? Or observed yourself learning a new way of doing things?

Isn't it interesting that, even though we'd love to be able to do it perfectly the first time, we almost never do? We try for a bit, fall back, try again, fall back again, and try a few more times before we get the hang of it and actually begin to be able to do it. Then we do it many more times before we can do it well.

Well, there's a reason for that: every time we learn something new we learn a significant part of it, but there's still more not yet learned. So we go thru the process again from the beginning to pick up the pieces. And each time we do, it's a little easier, a little less stress, a little more effective. Often there's a point where we're sure we'll never get it. Then, suddenly, we have it. We've changed from one Mental Framework to another and the new skill is now a part of us. As Emma Hopkins reminds us in *The Spiritual Science*, "it's not the practice that does the trick; it's the realization that it is part of us."[13]

The same is true with mastering the key to *The Secret*.

---

[13] From the Library of Hidden Knowledge series, *The Spiritual Science of Emma Curtis Hopkins*, Lesson 10.

We go through the process of expressing, releasing, and creating several times, as the issue comes up again.

Each time we see results: we see changes in ourselves and in the people and world around us. But after a while, for some reason we usually aren't aware of, we find ourselves feeling the same old feelings and experiencing many of the same kinds of things we were before.

It's so frustrating! Here we've done all this work and the old pattern is showing up again!

At that point we may feel like quitting. We may say to ourselves "this stuff doesn't really work for me." And many of my students have done just that!

Then they attend a group, or pick up one of the books, or simply stop and think about it: "Is it true that there's no progress?" "Haven't I experienced far more joy and far less distress than I used to?" "And really, it's only been a few days and I'm recognizing it, rather than going on for months!"

They begin realize how far they've truly come and they start the expressing and releasing process again, determined to create a new kind of life for themselves – one with even more joy and even less distress than they've been experiencing.

If we continue, if we do the process again – expressing the feelings; releasing the pattern; setting our intention; creating our new life, and continuing to affirm that new way of being – then an amazing discovery awaits us! We find that we haven't fallen nearly as far as we thought, we've made far more progress than we'd come to believe, and the world around us has changed far more than we ever thought was possible!

This is the nature of an iterative process.

We iterate through it and reiterate through it, and each time it's easier and shorter and less intense, until one day we realize that the event that used to trigger our old pattern and reactions didn't do that this time. If we do the process again at that point, we soon become aware that we never have that experience any more – the pattern is cleared from our Mental Framework and we are, truly, free to choose and experience the life we desire.

🗝 Key Eight: Discernment

Have you ever stood in front of a grocery case, looking at all the wonderful food, wondering how you would ever choose? Ever had difficulties deciding which gift to get for a beloved? Which book to read or video to watch next?

Most of us find ourselves facing these kinds of decisions on a regular basis without a clue as to how to make them.

Then there are the important decisions: which job to take, which house to move into, which person to get close to...

For many of us, the process of making decisions is so distressing that we take the easy way out and let the decision be made for us.

That, we find later, often leads to experiences we wish weren't happening!

Not Analysis

Some of us are very analytical about it. We make lists; we compare pros and cons; we invite input from our friends; we go online and find out what experts say. But when it comes down to it, only we can make the final choice, and all the data in the world can't guarantee it's the best one for us. In fact, it's a truism among experienced CEOs that "the data only takes you so far and then you have to trust your instinct."

This flies in the face of much of what we've been taught. Having been someone whose job it was to teach "decision-making" tools, believe me, I understand. I can tell you how to build decision matrices and do sensitivity analyses, how to assess risks and impacts, to build computer programs to test alternatives, and all kinds of other tools and techniques, but what has become absolutely clear is that all of them are, at best, ways to understand the interconnections of the world we live in, and, at worst, ways to justify the decisions that, somehow, we've already made.

Not Judgment

James Allen stresses the importance of discernment:

> Discernment, being a spiritual skill, can only be developed... by questioning, examining, and analyzing one's own ideas, opinions, and conduct. Our critical, fault-finding tendencies must no longer be applied to the opinions and conduct of others but must be applied—with no holds barred—to our own self. We must be prepared to question every one of our own opinions, thoughts, and behaviors and test them against our chosen principles...[14]

He tells us to let go of the habit of judging others for their actions in favor of really studying our own thoughts and actions so we can change them.

---

[14] From The Library of Hidden Knowledge series, *As We Think So We Are*, p. 74.

In *The Spiritual Science,* Emma Curtis Hopkins tells her students

> You must have ... discriminative knowledge to separate promptly and without error the ego-self human mind from the divine Awareness. You must separate any perceivable material formulation from the spiritually visible.... Would you say there were two boats because you saw a reflection of your boat in the water?[15]

To discern is not to judge someone or something as "good" or "bad", or even as "real" or "unreal"

It is simply to discover the extent to which what is in front of us is in alignment with our current intention.

That's it. That's all there is to it.

Learning to Discern

Learning how to go about it, however, may take some practice. Most of us don't have the faintest notion of how to know whether something is helpful or not, or whether it will move us in our desired direction. We've been trained, in our culture, not to pay attention to the subtle signals. We've been taught to think and act in the way that others – "experts", "authority figures" – tell us.

After my students have attended even a couple of sessions of my various classes, lectures, and support

---

[15] From The Library of Hidden Knowledge series, *The Spiritual Science of Emma Curtis Hopkins,* Lesson 6, p. 63.

groups, they all know about the "3Es". It's a kind of hallmark among the methods I offer.

Back in the 1990s, some Stanford business school professors wanted to know why and how the new breed of entrepreneurs that had built Silicon Valley were so effective. So, like all good academicians, they constructed a survey and interviewed a bunch of successful people, and they did some statistical measures and came up with some remarkable results. The book *Creativity in Business*, by Michael Ray and Rochelle Myers, summarizes the work.

What these very successful people told them was that they were most effective when they only did certain kinds of things. Those things had to be fun to do – that meant they were using their gifts and skills. It had to take almost no effort to do it – not that it might not be a lot of hard and challenging work, but that it wasn't something they had to make themselves do. And finally, these highly successful businessmen and women said that they only did the things that made them feel energized and ready to take on something more. When they did any other kinds of things they weren't nearly as effective, so they first checked to see if such tasks really needed to be done and, if they did, delegated them to people who were effective doing them.

As a consultant to small business owners and entrepreneurs, as well as a teacher and coach, I've found this work to be very helpful, and have used it so often that I've reduced their results into a simple formula:

$$E_f \Leftrightarrow 3E$$

It means:

Effective if and only if Enjoyable, Effortless, & Energizing

It's very simple, but somehow hard to grasp. I'm always intrigued to see which one of the Es a client or student can't remember! If they don't remember "Enjoyable" they're usually dealing with critical parent issues. If they can't remember "Energizing", they've typically been out of touch with their physical and emotional responses to situations. A few folks have a hard time remembering "Effortless." These generally have been trained to think "no pain; no gain" and a large part of our work is to help them find ways to work smarter; not harder.

All of them have found, though, that whenever they choose in the direction of the "3 Es" life flows wonderfully well.

Knowing whether it "fits"

Now let's go back to the original question in this chapter, "have you ever stood in front of a grocery case trying to decide...?" It's a common situation, and most of us have done so at some time, maybe in a bakery or ice cream shop or drive-thru, rather than a meat counter or deli, but most of us have had to choose what we were going to buy and eat at some point in our lives.

How do you know what to ask for?

Well, in the past, you might have chosen by some combination of price, quantity, familiarity, memory of past experiences with similar flavors, and whatever emotion you were bringing to the moment.

Now you're ready to choose based on what you intend your life to become, rather than being driven by the past and your beliefs about limitation.

So, remember, if you will, a case displaying various food items and imagine standing there knowing that what you choose will either move you in the direction of your intention or not. It will fit with who you are now, or not. It will support your life becoming the best it can be, or not.

That's a very different basis for choosing, isn't it?

There are as many ways to do this as there are people on the planet, but my students have come up with a few that work for them. These are simple and let the body-mind function as a whole, rather than as if it were split into separate intellectual, emotional, and physical components.

Checking the energy. Imagine that you can hold your hand in front of you, palm facing the case, and that your palm tingles or heats up when the food that fits this new version of you is in front of it. Now, in your imagination, hold your hand in front of the different-sized empty containers that are sitting nearby and "feel" which one is the size that works best today. Again, there will be a tingling or temperature change, or some other shift in how the hand feels.

Checking the muscle response. They may also use something called "muscle testing" or "applied kinesiology" (an inaccurate term for an effective technique!). The idea behind this method is that our muscles are strong around things that are in alignment with who we truly are and weaker when things are not. There are many variations in the use of the method, the most well-known being to hold something in one hand over the heart, extending the other arm out to have someone else push down on it. Others will hold something against their chest with both hands and sense whether their body tends to maintain balance or fall one direction or another (they usually stop before they fall). A very discrete version is to hold a finger against the thumb on one hand in a circle and try to pry them apart by spreading the 2nd and 3rd fingers of the other hand inside the circle. In all methods, holding strong means the item is a "fit" and weaker means it "doesn't fit" who you are right now, including your intentions for the future. This can be applied to anything from medications and foods to books and other entertainments to ideas.

Overall sensing. A third approach to discovering whether something fits who we are in our process of accomplishing our intended way of being is to simply sense how the body-mind reacts. Sometimes this is more easily done after we've used other methods to learn how to sense the fit, but we can all learn to "read" our own body-mind systems at very subtle levels.

> *Most of the time the body tenses up in response to distress, ready for "fight, flight, or freeze."*

Only occasionally, when we're faced with something we really want to do that will take some exertion, will it tense up as a positive response. So the fundamental question is "do I tense or relax?"

The next-level question is "do I have any negative sensations?" Is all well in the gut? In the heart area? In the head? Around the throat? In the weak spot where you've been injured or had some kind of illness or infection (maybe more than once)?

If any part of the body turns over, tightens up, hurts, or simply "tweaks" a little, it's a sign that what you're considering is not in alignment with who you are now and where you're heading.

Sensing the Light around it. Another thing to be aware of when considering whether something fits is to observe which of the objects (or people or jobs or whatever) seem to stand out, to have more energy, to be a little brighter – even to glow a bit. This test is described well in James Redfield's *The Celestine Prophecy*, and is often very effective. I use it a lot to decide which route to take on my frequent road trips.

Sensing the pull. Finally, and perhaps the simplest approach, is to observe whether there's any tendency in the body to move in a particular direction. This works really well when walking or driving, but may also help when there are several things in front of you to choose from. It feels as if a string or a magnet is pulling the body toward the direction that fits best.

You may have noticed that none of these methods involve any form of analysis or deep thinking. There's a reason for that:

> *The Mental Framework will get in the way much more often when you "figure it out" than when you simply let yourself "discover."*

Knowing when to quit

The same set of approaches can be used to help us know when we've done all that will be effective at this time: our body will tell us – if we allow ourselves to observe.

The signs will vary from person to person, but first there's usually a vague sense of "not okay" – of things not working properly, of ideas not flowing well, of losing track of what's going on – long before we usually begin to feel tired or complete with what we're focusing on. If we can learn to stop at that point, we'll continue to be effective. If not, we'll put more and more effort into what we're doing (ignoring one of the 3Es) until we can't continue focusing on it, and often make mistakes in the process.

So the first thing is to notice if it's still "effortless, enjoyable, and energizing." If it isn't, it's time to stop – if only for a minute or two, and focus on something else.

The next set of indicators, after we're no longer as effective as we might be, but before we're actually worn out, is that our body begins to call our attention. We may hurt somewhere or feel hungry, tired, or thirsty, or our favorite addiction might be calling us.

> *In spite of what most of us were taught growing up, this is not the time to keep plugging at something to get it done.*

This is time to stop, go inside, and discover what we really are ready to be doing right now, instead of this.

It may simply be to get up and stretch, do a couple pushups, or go for a walk around the block – or it may be to shift away from this process completely and focus on something entirely different – whatever it is,

> *we won't be effective until we're focused on what's really ours to be doing right now: what's effortless, enjoyable, and energizing NOW.*

🗝 Key Nine: Enjoyment

Accepting the fact that enjoyment is one of the ways we know whether some option or activity fits our intention is usually a challenge. After all, we've been taught "no pain; no gain," and other such maxims most of our lives.

The idea that we can move through life from one enjoyable experience to another sounds almost blasphemous!

And yet, if you think about it, isn't that what you're really longing for? Isn't that what a "heavenly life" would be? Having each day unfold in more and more joy and delight?

If that's the case, then how could we possibly get there by living a life that's full of experiences that are not enjoyable?

Abraham-Hicks' Contribution to the film The Secret

Two sets of teachings may be helpful here. One is from a teacher who was part of the original production of the film *The Secret*: the channeled entity known as Abraham. It turns out that when Rhonda Byrne got the idea for what she thought would be a television series shown in Australia, she taped it with Esther Hicks channeling Abraham as the centerpiece – and there are a few copies of that original pilot still floating around. Later, when they realized that it would have to be sold as a stand-alone video in the US, Abraham told Esther and her husband Jerry to separate themselves from the production, which they did. So most of us have seen the film without them in it.

The reason Byrne initially wanted to showcase Abraham-Hicks is because of the clarity of the teachings in the books and videos she had seen, such as *The Power of Deliberate Intent*. She found that, when Esther goes into trance and starts talking as Abraham, two very clear ideas are consistently and constantly presented:

(1) Everything we want already exists, simply because we've desired it, and

(2) They're all "downstream" from here – accessible by simply relaxing.

Other teachers have stated the first idea as "you can't desire something that doesn't already exist" or "your desires are the indication that those things are ready for you to experience them."

This is because we live in a much larger set of dimensions than the 3-dimensional world we see at any given moment (after all, the human eye can see only 1% of the electromagnetic spectrum!). Those other dimensions are outside of space and time. That means, like your hand touching two pages of this book at once, our larger dimensional-self can make connections between things we can't even imagine with our normal thinking in our limited universe. (To explore this idea more fully, try the works of Jane Roberts or read Richard Bach's *One*,) So, when we get an idea, it begins a process outside of space and time to make it part of our physical experience.

> *The things we desire are already taking form around us, ready for us to be ready to experience them.*

The second idea, that we need to "relax into" the desired experience, is sometimes stated (by Abraham and others, such as Penny Peirce in *Frequency*) as "raise your vibrations to the level of your desires." It's how we experience anything wonderful: we're relaxed, energized and joyful, just as we would be floating downstream in a beautiful setting.

> *When our energy and the energy of our desires match, we experience those desires and more.*

Other Inspirations for The Secret

The photocopy that inspired Byrne's transformation and the film that followed was Wallace Wattles' book *The Science of Getting Rich*. In it, Wattles encouraged his readers to stop worrying and fretting and to start thinking positively by practicing feeling the way we will when we actually achieve our desired intentions. He called it "thinking in a certain way." And he meant that word "certain" in both senses: as specific and unique, and also as predictable, sure, something you can count on. So he was saying the same thing: if you want to experience something wonderful, start feeling wonderful!

But, you ask, how can we feel wonderful when we don't have what we want?

The answer is twofold: imagination and anticipation.

Virtually all of the self-improvement teachers of the past 100 years have emphasized the importance of feeling good regardless of our circumstances.

They've all told us that the situation we're in is not the important thing; it's merely the result of what we've said, thought, and done in the past. What's important is what we're creating now. So we need to shift our attention from any disturbing circumstances and focus on what's most important to us, now.

To do this, they've encouraged us to take time away from others to imagine what it will be like when what we've desired has come to pass. And, as we noted earlier, researchers have demonstrated over the years that the body-mind can't tell the difference between a richly imagined experience and a physical event. In fact, the more senses we can bring into the imagined experience, the more powerful it is.

So, the teachers say, take some time every day to imagine, as fully as possible, every aspect of what it will be like when what you're intending for your life has come to pass. And this is what you've been doing as part of your Affirmation process in Key 8.

But there's something more needed if we're going to align our Mental Framework with the joy-filled life we desire; we need to recognize that, whether we can see it or not, it's on its way, and we need to feel the joyful anticipation of its arrival – just as new parents do when expecting that first baby. They can't see it but there are signs that it's on its way. And so it is with all we have intended – whether we've completed the process outlined in the book or not:

What we intend will come to pass. The trick is to intend only one thing; not the many things of our old, conflicting Mental Framework,

So we go through the process, acknowledging, expressing, and releasing the old thoughts and patterns, then replacing them with new ones and affirming the intention of living only in the new Framework.

From that place of conflict-free clarity, we can joyfully anticipate the unfolding of our desires. We do so, not because we've worked hard for them, but because we've relaxed into the process of their appearance in our lives, without effort, but enjoyably and energizingly.

Key Ten: Love and Appreciation

When we experience deep joy, we also experience a deep gratitude to the source of that joy, whether that source be another person, our Creator, whether we call it God or the Universal Process. The 2 feelings happen together, like 2 sides of a coin: joy and gratitude; appreciation and love; peace and contentment – all are aspects of the same experience.

When we've learned to choose what really gives us joy, released what has been blocking us from experiencing that joy, and learned to choose the 3Es in all our activities, then most of our life is enjoyable, and that same feeling of gratitude and appreciation becomes our norm.

Appreciation, with the love and peace and joy that are associated with it, is a high-frequency state of being which attracts and sustains high-frequency experiences.

It's a positive, reinforcing process: more joy means more gratitude and appreciation, which brings more joyful experiences, which brings more gratitude and appreciation, and so on.

When we feel this way, our life becomes magical. We hear ourselves saying "I can't believe..." or "This is unreal!"

Then we realize, No, this is Reality; the other way of being was a nightmare and now we are awake – and truly alive.

This is the epitome of the Law of Attraction at work. This is *The Secret*, unlocked.

Author's Biography

Ruth L Miller, Ph.D. is an eclectic scholar integrating ancient wisdom with modern science for a more harmonious future. In addition to the Library of Hidden Knowledge series, her many books include *Home – creating humanity's future; Making The World Go Away; Mary's Power – embracing the divine feminine as the age of Empire ends; Language of Life – finding answers to modern issues in an ancient way of speaking* (co-authored with Milt Markewitz); *Empowered Care – mind-body medicine methods* (co-authored with Robert Bruce Newman); *The Science of Mental Healing – New Thought in America,* and the Paths of Power series of biographies of New Thought teachers.

An ordained minister in the transcendentalist New Thought tradition of mental healing and transformation, Miller also holds degrees in anthropology, cybernetics, environmental studies, and systems science. Before ordination she worked as a college professor and a consulting futurist, and she continues to speak to a wide range of audiences about the individual and collective possibilities emerging as our culture is transformed. www.ruthlmillerphd.com

Current Titles in the Library of Hidden Knowledge*

As We Think, So We Are: James Allen's Guide to Transforming Our Lives

Natural Abundance: Ralph Waldo Emerson's Guide to Prosperity

One Law: Henry Drummond on Nature's Law, Spirit, and Love

The New Game of Life and How to Play It Florence Scovel Shinn's classic, updated for modern readers

The New Master Key System: Charles Haanel's classic, updated for modern readers

The New Science of Getting Rich: Wallace Wattles' classic, updated for modern readers

The Spiritual Science of Emma Curtis Hopkins

---

* Beyond Words Publishing, a division of Atira Books/Simon & Schuster: www.beyondword.com

www.ingramcontent.com/pod-product-compliance
Lightning Source LLC
Chambersburg PA
CBHW020145130526
44591CB00030B/237